MEMORIAL DAY

By EMMA CARLSON BERNE

Illustrations by SIMONE KRÜGER

Music by MARK MALLMAN

CANTATA
LEARNING

WWW.CANTATALEARNING.COM

CANTATA LEARNING

Published by Cantata Learning
1710 Roe Crest Drive
North Mankato, MN 56003
www.cantatalearning.com

Library of Congress Cataloging-in-Publication Data
Names: Berne, Emma Carlson, author. | Krüger, Simone, illustrator.
Title: Memorial Day / by Emma Carlson Berne ; illustrated by Simone Krüger ;
  music by Mark Mallman.
Description: North Mankato, MN : Cantata Learning, [2018] | Series: Holidays
  in rhythm and rhyme | Audience: Grades K–3. | Audience: Ages 5–7. |
Identifiers: LCCN 2017017548 (print) | LCCN 2017018477 (ebook) | ISBN
  9781684101610 (ebook) | ISBN 9781684101375 (hardcover : alk. paper) | ISBN
  9781684101931 (pbk. : alk. paper)
Subjects: LCSH: Memorial Day--Juvenile literature.
Classification: LCC E642 (ebook) | LCC E642 .B49 2018 (print) | DDC
  394.262--dc23
LC record available at https://lccn.loc.gov/2017017548

978-1-68410-389-8 (hardcover)

Book design and art direction, Tim Palin Creative
Editorial direction, Kellie M. Hultgren
Music direction, Elizabeth Draper
Music arranged and produced by Mark Mallman

ACCESS THE MUSIC!

SCAN CODE WITH MOBILE APP

CANTATALEARNING.COM

Printed in the United States   4303

TIPS TO SUPPORT LITERACY AT HOME

WHY READING AND SINGING WITH YOUR CHILD IS SO IMPORTANT

Daily reading with your child leads to increased academic achievement. Music and songs, specifically rhyming songs, are a fun and easy way to build early literacy and language development. Music skills correlate significantly with both phonological awareness and reading development. Singing helps build vocabulary and speech development. And reading and appreciating music together is a wonderful way to strengthen your relationship.

READ AND SING EVERY DAY!

TIPS FOR USING CANTATA LEARNING BOOKS AND SONGS DURING YOUR DAILY STORY TIME

1. As you sing and read, point out the different words on the page that rhyme. Suggest other words that rhyme.

2. Memorize simple rhymes such as Itsy Bitsy Spider and sing them together. This encourages comprehension skills and early literacy skills.

3. Use the questions in the back of each book to guide your singing and storytelling.

4. Read the included sheet music with your child while you listen to the song. How do the music notes correlate to the words of the song?

5. Sing along on the go and at home. Access music by scanning the QR code on each Cantata book. You can also stream or download the music for free to your computer, smartphone, or mobile device.

Devoting time to daily reading shows that you are available for your child. Together, you are building language, literacy, and listening skills.

Have fun reading and singing!

On Memorial Day we remember the US **soldiers** who fought and died in wars. This holiday is **observed** on the last Monday in May.

After the US **Civil War**, people went to the **cemetery** on a special day each year. They visited with other families and decorated the **graves** of family members who had died in the war. This day was called Decoration Day. Later, the name was changed to Memorial Day.

On Memorial Day, people go to parades and **ceremonies**. Sometimes they have picnics. Many kids are done with school, so people think of Memorial Day as the start of summer.

Let's sing about Memorial Day together!

The school year is done! It's the end of May.
Ready to honor Memorial Day?

We'll hoist up the flag and raise it high.
Proudly we'll let the colors fly.

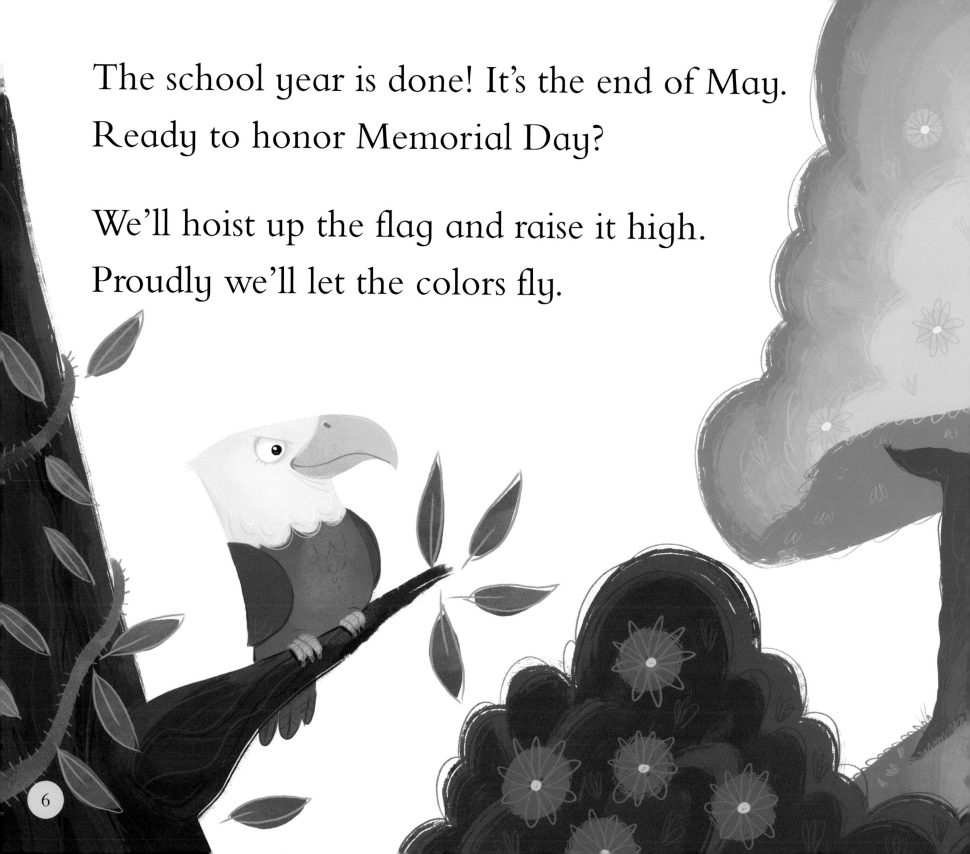

For freedom, clap your hands,
for soldiers in our land.

They fought for us,
so we'd be free.

For freedom, clap your hands.

The parade is coming, I hear the **tramping**,
footsteps draw nearer, boots are stamping.

Veterans march, all in a line,
their heads held high, their medals shine.

For freedom, clap your hands,
for soldiers in our land.

They fought for us,
so we'd be free.

For freedom, clap your hands.

That isn't all, for summer is here.
The pool is ready. Give a big cheer!

Put on your suit and make a dash.
See who makes the biggest splash.

For freedom, clap your hands,
for soldiers in our land.

They fought for us,
so we'd be free.

For freedom, clap your hands.

Summertime starts on Memorial Day.
We can't wait to go out to run and play.

But first on this day we'll honor the brave.
We won't forget the lives they gave.

For freedom, clap your hands,
for soldiers in our land.

They fought for us,
so we'd be free.

For freedom, clap your hands.

SONG LYRICS
Memorial Day

The school year is done! It's the end of May.
Ready to honor Memorial Day?
We'll hoist up the flag and raise it high.
Proudly we'll let the colors fly.

For freedom, clap your hands,
for soldiers in our land.
They fought for us,
so we'd be free.
For freedom, clap your hands.

The parade is coming, I hear the tramping,
footsteps draw nearer, boots are stamping.
Veterans march, all in a line,
their heads held high, their medals shine.

For freedom, clap your hands,
for soldiers in our land.
They fought for us,
so we'd be free.
For freedom, clap your hands.

That isn't all, for summer is here.
The pool is ready—give a big cheer!
Put on your suit and make a dash.

See who makes the biggest splash.

For freedom, clap your hands,
for soldiers in our land.
They fought for us,
so we'd be free.

For freedom, clap your hands.
Summertime starts on Memorial Day.
We can't wait to go out to run and play.
But first on this day we'll honor the brave.
We won't forget the lives they gave.

For freedom, clap your hands,
for soldiers in our land.
They fought for us,
so we'd be free.
For freedom, clap your hands.

Memorial Day

Children's Patriotic
Mark Mallman

Verse

1. The school year is done! It's the end of May. Read-y to hon-or Me-mo-ri-al Day? We'll

hoist up the flag and raise it high. Proud-ly we'll let the col-ors fly.

Chorus

For free-dom, clap your hands, for sol-diers in our land. They fought for us, so we'd be free. For

free-dom, clap your hands.

Verse 2
The parade is coming, I hear the tramping,
footsteps draw nearer, boots are stamping.
Veterans march, all in a line,
their heads held high, their medals shine.

Chorus

Verse 3
That isn't all, for summer is here.
The pool is ready. Give a big cheer!
Put on your suit and make a dash.
See who makes the biggest splash.

Chorus

Verse 4
Summertime starts on Memorial Day.
We can't wait to go out to run and play.
But first on this day we'll honor the brave.
We won't forget the lives they gave.

Chorus

GLOSSARY

cemetery—the place where people who have died are buried

ceremonies—activities people do to mark a special day or time

Civil War—a war fought from 1861 to 1865 between US states

graves—the places in the ground where people who have died are buried, marked with a stone

observed—marked or honored a special day or time

soldiers—people who serve in armies

tramping—loud, rhythmic walking

veterans—people who used to be soldiers

GUIDED READING ACTIVITIES

1. Memorial Day celebrates two things: the soldiers who helped our country and the unofficial start of summer. Can you think of another holiday that has two meanings?

2. Parades are one way of celebrating Memorial Day. What is another way we remember soldiers on this holiday?

3. Did you have or do you have soldiers in your family? If they lived a long time ago, where are they buried?

TO LEARN MORE

Bailey, R. J. *Memorial Day*. Minneapolis: Bullfrog Books, 2017.

Messner, Kate. *Rolling Thunder*. New York: Scholastic, 2017.

Walsh, Barbara E. *The Poppy Lady: Moina Belle Michael and Her Tribute to Veterans*. Honesdale, PA: Calkins Creek, 2012.